YOU ARE STRONGER THAN YOUR SITUATIONS:

PLEASE DON'T JUMP

YOU *are* STRONGER THAN YOUR SITUATIONS

PLEASE DON'T JUMP

DELORIS E. JORDAN

Jordan Signature Publishing, Inc

Elkins Park, PA 19027

You Are Stronger Than Your Situations: Please Don't Jump
© 2020 by Deloris E. Jordan

Published by Jordan Signature Publishing, Inc, P.O. Box 26743, Elkins Park, PA 19027

Edited by Liberty Baker, Affordable Christian Editing
Cover Design by Deloris E. Jordan and Vanessa Mendozzi
Cover photos by Cherise Richards Photography – www.cheriserichardsphotography.com
Interior Book Design by VMC Art & Design, LLC

Library of Congress Control Number: 2019908209

ISBN: 978-0-9714472-1-9 (hardcover)
ISBN: 978-0-9714472-2-6 (paperbook)
ISBN: 978-0-9714472-3-3 (ebook)

This book is dedicated to all you marvelously complex individuals who have yet to realize just how much God loves you and how intentional He was with gifting you life.

ACKNOWLEDGMENTS

As always, my literary sharing is made possible by my redeeming Savior Jesus Christ and my three beautiful children, who have loved me unconditionally through some very difficult days. I will be forever grateful Cori, Sheri, and Bree, that God chose me to be your mother.

One of the remarkable things about God, and there are many, is that He never leaves us to bear our burdens alone. In addition to being ever so ready to walk alongside us Himself, He often provides earthly souls to walk alongside us as well. Aunt Fannie is one such person in my life. A staunch believer in my sanity when others around me questioned it, thankfully she remains just a phone call away when I need earthly affirmation. Ninety years old now, she and her daughter Lee, who I have adopted as my big sister, often beckons me home so that they can shower me with hugs. In addition to their comfort, I am blessed to be surrounded these days with a surplus of family and friends whom I dare not attempt to name here. I would undoubtedly omit someone inadvertently and cause them to think they are not important to me. In actuality, I thank all of you for loving and supporting me in my journey of wellness.

Thank you to Liberty Baker, who began praying for me and this book before editing one word of it. I came to value your opinion so much that I found myself seeking your thoughts on other aspects of it even when your work on it had long been completed. Thank you so much for enduring me. Likewise, thank you Vanessa Mendozzi, Victoria Colotta, and Gary Nyenhuis for helping to bring this book to life. To God be the glory!

TABLE OF CONTENTS

NOTE TO MY READERS...

I n that few of us walk around analyzing our strength and endurance, chances are that few of us truly know the depth of our capabilities. Life has a way of testing our resilience, however, with experiences that many of us would never willingly embrace on our own. Situations that many of us would deem impossible to withstand or to overcome.

Of all the challenges in my life that I regarded as insurmountable, the ability to survive my dark moments was at the top of my list. The ability to survive them with my sanity intact was a close second. With no expectations of surviving, I also never envisioned possessing any authentic joy in my life either. It all seemed so farfetched and implausible achievements to strive for that for many years I came to care little about being victorious in such efforts.

Today I am elated to say, however, that I not only achieved the milestone of surviving difficulties that I once thought to be unsurvivable but along the way I also came to be grateful for each heartrending situation that labored me with the burdensome task of living through them. I am not so appreciative that I would ever want to relive those arduous experiences again, however. But I am grateful enough to respect the lessons I gleaned from them, having walked away from each encounter stronger and wiser than I ever expected to be.

But I did not survive those trying times so that I could write about them. I write about them *because* I survived them. Undoubtedly, God knew each time He intervened and thwarted my suicidal efforts that He would one day use me and those dark moments in my life to encourage you to believe in your own resilience. And to believe, likewise, in His ability to also get you to the other side of your dark times too—to joy!

Such is the purpose of this book!

As I write to you now under the ushering of Christ, let me acknowledge at the onset of our time together that I am not a therapist, psychologist, or anyone that possesses any academic knowledge on the subject of suicide. I am merely an individual who stumbled to the edge of a life that I did not want or know how to live and jumped off into the dark mystery of suicide.

And survived!

I did not survive just my suicidal attempts, however. I survived all of the painful situations that once made suicide such an attractive solution—the sexual abuse that raided my childhood, the fragmented adult life that resulted from the violation, the years of rejection that came from my mother and later my family after disclosing the abuse—the profound shame that came to be the measuring stick by which I evaluated my worth, the lack of knowledge to fix all that was wrong with me, and my vanquished mindset to even try.

Having written transparently of those anguishes in my first book, *In My Family's Shadow*, I dare not burden either of our spirits by recounting them again here in detail. I do share within these pages, however, tidbits of situations that led me to believe that my life was insignificant and had no purpose. More importantly, I share with you how I came to learn that much of what I thought about my life was far from true. Not only was my life worth living, but it was also full of purpose. As was my pain!

Before delving into all of that, however, let me first share with you how I came to be writing this book. Its sheer existence illustrates how God is a *plan-interrupter* unlike any other. I am not sure if that is even a word, but it is a true characteristic of God nonetheless. And as you will come to see, He has interrupted several of my plans on more than one occasion.

Like most people who come to realize the emancipation of writing once they have crossed the threshold of authoring their first book, I have begun several manuscripts over the years, ranging in topic from abuse to foreclosure. But having become the most mentally and emotionally healthiest that I have ever been in my life, my most recent focus had been on completing a book that saluted my wellness. Having made it to the other side of darkness, no longer trying to kill myself, run from my life, or fear it even, I felt empowered and wanted to use that empowerment to speak strength into the lives of those who find themselves struggling to live. So embracing the same six-word declaration that God often proclaimed to me during times when I swore I did not have the strength to take another step in my onerous life, I titled my new book, *You Are Stronger Than Your Situations*.

Although not at all what I had desired to hear from God during harrowing moments, I eventually became so enamored with the strength-inducing declaration that I not only used it as the title of my book, but I also used its acronym, YASTYS, as the name for my online merchandising store. Passionately embraced now as my personal mantra, I often text it or its acronym to family and friends to remind them of their resilience.

With my first book having shone a light into the darkest crevices of my life, my new book was set to reflect on how my life had changed as a result of *In My Family's Shadow's* illumination. How God had used it as the catalyst in helping me to not only face the truth of my life but to take ownership of it and make peace with it. Those three huge endeavors did not happen easily or without grave consequences, however.

In addition to celebrating my survival of it all, my new book would also grant me the opportunity to encourage other individuals struggling with hardships not unlike my own. Of course being Michael Jordan's sister encumbers my life with a few difficulties that most people will never encounter. But once you exclude that factor, however, my adversities are very much like those that individuals experiencing a spirit of brokenness face daily. Brokenness that I know well and can speak on profoundly.

As is often the case with life-enriching endeavors, my effort to complete my YASTYS manuscript was met with a steady stream of distractions that diverted my attention away from it once it was near completion.

Today, I am wholeheartedly convinced that when negative hindrances no longer impede our life as they once did, Satan is not at all shy about using *good* distractions to sidetrack us as well. Subtle little obstacles that at first may not appear to be hindrances at all, but over time succeed in luring us away from tasks that once held our attention. Anything to keep us from doing and becoming all that God has purposed for us to do and become.

I knew writing the book was something that God had laid on my heart to do. Each time I turned my attention to the task, however, another *good* hindrance came along to distract me—a new job, a unique business opportunity, and new adventures even—all wonderful things but distractions just the same.

In early March of 2019, with the snow season winding down and the claustrophobia of winter hibernation setting in, my two daughters and I began to crave a change of scenery. With my birthday soon to arrive in April, my girls began a steady stream of inquiries as to how we would celebrate it. Set to turn 60, there was no way my oldest daughter Sheri, the event-planning connoisseur of the family, was going to let such a milestone pass by in my life without some sort of celebration. Having teamed up with her two siblings to host a surprise party for my 50th birthday, she wanted this momentous birthday to be no less eventful. Especially given that for my 59th, I had slipped away to San Diego, rented a villa, a convertible, and cruised the west coast for a week. An adventure that initially frightened me because I had never done anything like that before, and knew nothing at all about the west coast. Once I pushed past all of those fears, however, I had a wonderful time.

Liberated by my adventure to a new degree, I became a travel junkie for the remainder of the year. So much so that my sister declared that it was as if all anyone had to do was broach the subject of traveling and I was packed, ready to go.

She was right and my bulging credit card balances can attest to that. But having raised my three children to the point of being an empty nester, my San Diego caper had awakened me to a newfound love of fun traveling—traveling that did not involve work. And although I took time out of my San Diego adventure to visit a women's shelter there, talking and sharing with the women was just as encouraging for me as it was for them. I love opportunities that allow me to plant seeds of encouragement. I never view them as work.

Nonetheless, bitten by the traveling bug, I racked up quite a few frequent flyer miles that year with trips to California, Dubai, and Greece in between. So when my daughters pressed me to decide on how I wanted to celebrate my 60th birthday, my mind once turned again to traveling and I opted for a girl's trip to Arizona. I am not sure why it was on my bucket list, but it was and we went!

Once there, the girls and I had a wonderful time together.

Unfortunately, their work schedule only allowed them a 4-day long weekend excursion while mine allowed me a longer stay. Seizing the opportunity to do a little Arizona cruising like I had done in California the year before, once the girls were on their flights heading home, I swapped our leased SUV for a convertible sports car. And with eager anticipation, I looked forward to beginning a new adventure the following morning.

The next morning, however, I awakened to find myself grappling with an unsettling mood that I could not shake. Engulfed by a grave feeling of dejection that came out of the blue, I struggled to pinpoint its origin. Although I missed the girls, especially Sheri's six-month-old daughter, Zoe, I was not only accustomed to living alone, I was also comfortable with it. Yet, between lying down the night before and rising this particular morning, a confusing sadness had overtaken me.

Turning to the only place that I know to take my questions, pains, and troubles these days, I turned to God seeking help for my aggrieved spirit. But neither prayer nor devotional reading lifted my melancholy mood, however. So turning to the other outlet that often brings me relief, I began to write out my emotions. And as God would have it to be, my journaling then led to me working on my manuscript and for the duration of my time in Arizona, writing consumed me.

It was as if God had had enough of my distractions and was using my extended time in Arizona to realign my focus to the task that I had shelved much too long. Seemingly confined to the home office of the beautiful Airbnb that Sheri had leased, I no longer lounged by its pool or reveled in its lovely backyard oasis.

As for the convertible? It sat motionless in the garage as my daily routine became eating breakfast, reading my devotionals, then trotting off down the hall to the office where I would often remain until nightfall. Some days not even bothering to take a lunch or bathroom break. And by the time I said goodbye to Arizona, my original manuscript had been sliced, diced, and significantly altered to the point of it becoming a YASTYS series, with the first book of the series focused on suicide.

Talk about dumbfounded, I was stunned!

Talk about God being a plan-interrupter?

Oh yeah—in more ways than one!

> *"Many are the plans in a person's heart, but it is the LORD's purpose that prevails."*
> —Proverbs 19:21 NIV

Not only had I never contemplated writing a book series, but I also had never considered writing a book on the subject of suicide. Indeed a topic worthy of in-depth discussions, especially given the recent upsurge of individuals now embracing it to escape their pain, I just had never felt compelled to write about it outside of having disclosed my personal experience with it in my first book.

Keenly aware of my academic limitations, coupled with my belief that I had nothing valuable to say on the matter, I initially fought against all guiding thoughts of writing this book by reminding God of my shortcomings as well.

"Lord, you know that I do not know anything about suicide beyond my own experience with it," I declared as I proceeded to list all of the reasons why I was unqualified to even broach the subject.

"And to be quite honest, Lord, I have grown to be extremely grateful that I had failed in my suicide attempts. So how in the world can I write a book on it?" I queried God once I realized the direction that my writing had taken me. It was only after reading and meditating on a passage below from one of my daily devotionals that I came to understand the task that God had laid at my feet:

I AM THE TRUTH—unchanging, transcendent Truth! Many, many people believe that truth is relative—to the situation, the person, the day. But only absolute truth can provide a firm foundation for your life. Everything else is shifting sand.

Because I am inerrant Truth, *all of the treasures of wisdom and knowledge* are hidden in Me. You can find everything you need in your relationship with Me. I provide the foundation on which to build your life, and I Myself *am* Life. So the closer you live to Me, the more alive you will feel!

Many people struggle with issues of identity, wondering who they really are and what they're supposed to be doing with their lives. But the more fully you know Me—*the Truth*— the better you can understand yourself and the meaning of your life. So make every effort to know Me as I truly am. Also, *be prepared* to tell others about the Savior who has redeemed you and set you free.[1]

—Sarah Young

So here I am with my plans interrupted again, earnestly testifying of how I came to embrace a life that I once did not want. Having redeemed me from my days of pursuing death, God is not asking me to save you. For He and I both know that I am far too inept to even attempt such a thing. What He is asking of me, and what I am grateful to have the opportunity to do, however, is speak to what I have come to learn about His saving grace. Surrendered to that task with the writing of this book, it is my sincere hope that you will harvest from it, comfort and insight that inspires you to permit God to help you overcome all of the situations that are bankrupting your life and prompting you to give up— even to the point of contemplating suicide in some cases.

If turning to God does not appeal to you at the moment, that's okay. He was not always my first choice either. Over time, however, He taught me that I could trust Him. If you keep an open mind to that possibility as you journey through my experience with Him, hopefully, you will come to believe that you can trust Him too. At the very least, I hope you will come to better understand why I am so passionate about Him now and also come to realize that you are not alone in your quest to better understand your life and self-worth.

Once resigned to the fact that suicide was not going

to be the solution for all that aggrieved me, and that I was indeed going to have to live out my story, I sought words of encouragement wherever I could find them. Though an avid reader of the Bible, I also found illuminating words of wisdom and consoling comfort in other thought-provoking books as well. I have sprinkled nuggets from a few of them throughout this book, similar to the one below. Hopefully, all of our efforts, collectively, will compel you to give considerable thought to the amazing possibilities your future holds—provided that you do not give up on living.

FIXIN' TO FIGHT

THERE WILL BE TIMES IN YOUR life when you face the unthinkable: when your worst fear comes to life, and you feel circumstances conspiring against you. Fear will threaten to overtake you. All light of hope will fade or barely flicker.

Refuse to give in to this fear. Giving in to trepidation shuts down your mind. Instead, fix your thoughts not on the threat but on the One who is all-powerful and stands with you. Fix your mind on God. And fight.

Some treasures are worth the fight. God decided **YOU** were one of them. He moved heaven and earth to save you, battled all the powers of hell arrayed against Him, and defeated the last enemy—death—to win your soul. God is a fighter. You are worth the fight. Your family, your home are worth the fight.

When you're up against fright or worry, focus your thinking on God's mighty power working for you. Remember His deliverance in your life in times past, and count on Him to help you now. Refuse to give up. Refuse to believe the despair. Fill your mind with His majestic authority. Seek His help. Then stand and fight.[2]

—The Authors

CHAPTER ONE

Marked In Utter Seclusion

"Each soil has had its own history. Like a river, a mountain, a forest, or any natural thing, its present condition is due to the influences of many things and events of the past."
–Charles Kellogg, The Soils That Support Us, 1956

I magine you and I sitting at the kitchen table—mine or yours—sharing a pot of coffee as we talk candidly about present hardships in our lives that, like soil, have been largely influenced by events from our past. From the dark circles under our eyes and the frown lines running freely across our foreheads, it is clear to see that life has left its mark. From work dilemmas to marital woes, parenting hardships to strained finances and relationships, we all find ourselves at times questioning whether or not we have the energy to keep pushing forward. With a steady stream of afflictions assailing our peace, it feels as if flickers of hope within us are steadily being extinguished. Some days, it takes all of the strength that we can muster to hold things together as we grip the seams of our lives.

Well acquainted with all of the above dilemmas and more myself, I have come to appreciate comforts gained from other individuals when they share stories of hardships with me. *Survivor* testaments that allow me to know that I am not alone in my experiences while testifying to the fact that if they survived, it is not so far-fetched to think that maybe I can too. Testimonies that encourage me to hold on a little longer, dig a little deeper, and perhaps trust God's guidance a little more. Stories that inspire me to endure the process that God is using to help me grow into the person He always purposed me to become.

As you and I gather at the kitchen table with our coffee and frown lines, I am more cognizant now than ever before that as intentional as God was with our race, gender, ethnicity, and hair texture even, He created both of us with specific purposes in mind as well. Purposes so unique and distinct that no one else in the universe can do that *thing* He created us to do. And no matter how similar our tasks may be, there is something so significantly different about them that I can never do yours the way you do them, reaching the same people you can reach, conveying the same message in the manner that God created you to do it. That fact is the same for every person.

With billions of people on this earth, each possessing

their own unique purpose, doesn't the perplexity of that fact just blow your mind?

Growing steadily into the person God purposed me to be, I am constantly learning and discovering new things about myself that I had never recognized or considered. One such thing is my fondness for encouragement. While I like receiving it, I find that I am far more fond of sharing it.

Drawn to that characteristic like a moth to a flame, I love speaking hope into other people's broken places, shining light into their dark times, and sharing words of strength during their not-so-strong moments. I love rallying them forward when they are declaring, "I can't" words of defeat, and I love rejoicing with them as they celebrate "Yes, I can" moments when they are triumphant in tests of endurance.

Invigorated by this now-realized attribute, it is clear to me that I was created to do this very thing but can in no way take credit for the characteristic. God destined it, and all of the events that led to it being part of my story, long before I was even aware of my existence. Psalm 139:14-16 (NLT) states that fact better than I ever could; *"You watched me as I was being formed in utter seclusion, as I was woven together in the dark of the womb. You saw me before I was born. Every day of my life was recorded in your book. Every moment laid out before a single day had passed."*

When I was not yet aware of my strengths, was deeply immersed in my brokenness, and struggling laboriously with my adversities, God was weaving all of my broken pieces together into a blanket of useful testimonies that He knew He would one day use for the good that could come from them. And although I saw nothing of value in me as a person, no purpose for my life, and was immensely resentful that He was preserving it when I so definitively did not want it, God knew it all had purpose.

His purpose!

Whispering into my spirit that I was strong enough to withstand all that He was allowing to affect my life, some days I was crying too hard to hear God. Other days I heard Him but was too irate with Him to listen. Knocked to my knees by an onslaught of unrelenting situations, I was eventually forced to seek Him for answers that He alone had. Once yielded to Him, I came to learn of a fundamental promise that He makes in Jeremiah 29:11-14 (MSG) to all who seek Him earnestly;

I know what I'm doing. I have it all planned out. Plans to take care of you; to not abandon you. Plans to give you the future you hope for. When you call on me, when you come and pray to me, I'll listen. When you come looking for me, you'll find me. Yes, when you get serious about finding me and want it more than anything else, I'll make sure you won't be disappointed. I'll turn things around for you.

As you face your own difficulties, you too may be feeling as if some of the things that God is using to chisel you into who He wants you to become are driving you to what you are positive will be your breaking point. And like me, there are most certainly days when you want no parts of Him. Especially if His remedy for ridding you of pain seems to be laden with *more* pain.

Already hurting, what rational person would willingly embrace more pain as a solution?

If the truth be told, many of us would rather live with our present afflictions than do the difficult work of ridding ourselves of it.

Believe me, I understand that inclination!

Several years ago, I was involved in a car accident with my son and sustained multiple injuries. Of all my injuries, it was a hand injury that caused me the most pain. Broken in several places at the wrist to the point of it just dangling, its pain was insanely intense. So much so that I flat out refused to allow the EMTs who responded to the scene of the accident to treat the injury. Upon arriving at the hospital, I continued that same attitude of defiance by refusing to allow the emergency room physicians address the injury as well.

I know! How can they help my hand if I refuse to allow them to touch it, right?

The pain was so excruciating that I was wholeheartedly convinced that anyone touching it would only amplify it. With that belief at the forefront of my thoughts, I instructed the doctors to focus on my other injuries and to bypass my hand altogether. Seeming to heed my directives, the two ER physicians turned their attention to my other injuries. With their focus now diverted away from my hand, I turned my attention to the nurses who were cutting off my jeans to assess my other injuries.

So engrossed in what was happening with the nurses, given that it is difficult to focus on little else when someone is cutting off your clothes, I completely missed the unspoken collaboration the two physicians had seemingly made with each other regarding my hand. And when I least expected it and was utterly unprepared for it, one doctor swiftly lifted my injured hand off my chest, aligned it with my arm, and held it in place while the other doctor put a splint on it.

Yes, that very hand that I had forbidden them to touch!

Convinced that I would die from the indescribable pain raking over my body, I could do little else but cry out uncensored. Enraged, I began to bitterly question the doctors in between my groans and tears, insistent on learning if they somehow knew me. Had I done something to either of them previously that I was unaware of that was prompting them to use this opportunity to seek revenge on me?

Now you and I both know that these doctors were really just trying to help me. But as is sometimes the case, help does not always feel good and may even cause us more pain, *temporarily*.

Following God is just like that!

Possessing the power to spare us all of life's afflictions, sometimes God chooses instead to allow us to stumble head-first down paths that overwhelm us and push us to dire moments of despair. But why should we, who are full of sin, be exempt from our trials when Jesus, who was without sin, was not?

And though He knew His Father's wondrous plan to restore His life three days after the trial of His crucifixion, Jesus still became *"sorrowful and deeply distressed"* as God's plan unfolded. So much so that the Bible declares that He prayed to His Father on three separate occasions to be spared the fate of the cross.

I believe that with His initial prayer, He merely asked to be spared the unmerciful fate. But I believe that with His second prayer, however, He prayed with far more urgency because the Bible says in Luke 22:43-44 (NIV) that *"An angel from heaven appeared to him and strengthened him. And being in anguish, he prayed more earnestly."*

If Jesus needed to be strengthened, can there be any doubt or surprise that you and I need to be encouraged and strengthened from time to time too? As you take a moment to ponder that thought, admit to yourself if not to anyone else, that until confronted with challenging moments, we have no other way of learning the true depth of our capabilities?

That truth is best illustrated with two news reports in which individuals were profiled for strength that they did not know they possessed until life challenged them in ways that they had never been challenged.

In one report, a young woman found the strength to lift a burning truck off of her father who was trapped underneath it. In the second report, a young boy who was not much larger than his younger brother had the astuteness and strength to catch the infant as he rolled off the changing table. In both instances, these accidental heroes won our praises and undoubtedly startled themselves in the process, with might and agility that neither probably realized they possessed until their situation beckoned those attributes out of hiding. I dare to say that like them, you too may not be aware of your own attributes until they are pointed out to you, or until life summons them forth!

For example, you look at you every day without seeing anything special about yourself. Then, in a span of a few short days, several strangers comment on how beautiful your eyes are; awakening you to their color, their bright sparkle, and their cute little slant. What changed; your eyes or your perception of them?

If someone referencing your eyes, or your work ethics, or even something as trivial as how well you waxed your car fills you with confidence and a new appreciation for the attribute, how might you feel if someone spoke words of endurance into your spirit?

Might that help you to become more cognizant of your inner strength as well?

Might you then come to realize that you are indeed stronger than the situations that are presently plaguing your life?

IF FEELINGS COULD TALK

IF YOUR FEELINGS COULD TALK, WHAT would they say?

Like children who blurt out whatever is on their minds, feelings convey the very contents of our souls—I am deeply loved. I'm ugly. No one cares. Life is beautiful. Things are going my way. I'm trapped and all alone. Life is unfair.

Those messages and those beliefs may or may not be true; they may or may not reflect reality. But they are there, and deep inside we have reasons for coming to those conclusions.

All of this provides an opportunity for God to reveal His truth. As you come into His presence and let your feelings talk, you hold those buried messages up to Him, and, if you can, you tell Him how you came to your conclusions. Then you look up into the face of God and ask, "Is it true? Am I really ugly? Will I really never amount to anything? What is the truth?"

That is when the transformation comes. That is when you learn the soul-cleansing truth. It is the truth for you and for all of us. We really are beautiful, deeply loved, fully capable sons and daughters of God.[3]

—The Authors

RELAX, MY CHILD, I'm in control. Let these words wash over you repeatedly, like soothing waves on a beautiful beach, assuring you of My endless love...Remember that you are My beloved. I am on your side and I want what is best for you...As you look ahead into the unknown future, relax in the knowledge of who you are—the one I love.[4]

—Sarah Young

CHAPTER TWO

The Pathway To Becoming

In my kitchen, taped on the wall most visible from my favorite reading area, is a portrait of a pair of hands kneading a vessel of clay. Right above the hands are the words, *"He is the potter, I am the clay."* Under the working hands, the words below complete the quote:

"I was just a lump of clay! Without a voice or the mind to know the reason why the Potter created me. But I am certain of this one thing; He indeed had a reason and in time will reveal it to me—if—I let Him."

There is nothing fancy about my latest piece of artwork. It is not painted with bright colors or any real artistic flair. Known to plaster walls in my home with sticky notes of encouragement at any given time, this particular day I elected to add visuals to the words for an extra dose of inspiration. And in that I am not an artist by any stretch of anyone's imagination, I downloaded a photo from the internet that best represented the image that was stirring in my spirit and inlaid my thoughts above the graphics where I thought them to be most impactful. Then, printing out my newest creation, I hastily hung it on the wall without bothering to frame it.

Despite the simplicity of my masterpiece, however, its declaration coupled with the dirty hands working the clay serves as my constant reminder that God is not yet finished working on me. On days when my tribulations have no rhyme or reason, the picture reminds me that my struggles are not fruitless regardless of how laborious they may be.

It is almost impossible to embrace godly perspectives, however, when confronted daily with the multitude of horrific events that are steadily becoming part of our global landscape. It is even more challenging to consider, embrace, and appreciate God when it is your life that is being intimately affected by the events. And while He may not be inflicting the hardships on us Himself, He is most certainly aware of them and more than capable of preventing them if He chooses to do so. Proverbs 15:3 (KJV) declares, "*The eyes of the LORD are in every place, beholding the evil and the good.*" Yet, in many instances, God remains silent as if He is oblivious to it all.

To the loving father who could barely contain his

excitement when he surprised his teenage son with a shiny new automobile for his high school graduation present, it is almost incomprehensible for him to believe that God allowed that same son to die tragically a few days later, in what came to be a mangled heap of fiberglass that was once an exciting gift.

To the family of the friendly neighbor who was always the first to welcome newcomers to the neighborhood with a warm smile and extended hand of friendship, it is unbearable to view God as loving, while yet understanding that He stood by and watched as a newcomer's son brutally murdered that same friendly neighbor late one night as she slept in her bed.

To a police officer who offered a colleague a ride home after a turbulent night of policing Philadelphia streets, it is difficult to fathom that God watched as the colleague turned down the lift home only to be slain a few short blocks from the precinct. Murdered for no other heart-wrenching reason than the fact that he wanted to walk so that he could inhale the fresh air of the new brisk morning that God Himself had created.

To a woman frozen in time to a younger period in her life that stripped her of innocence and childhood dreams, it would be many years before she could be convinced that God loved her, or was mindful of her even. To know that He had silently watched as she was being sexually abused by a father she adored, tormented by a mother that found it difficult to love her, and birthed into a family where she never quite fit in—how could anyone ever expect her to make sense of it all? Or, that the same God watched as she plotted her escape from it all by way of death?

I was twenty-three years old the first time I wrapped my brain around the thought of suicide. Having become convinced that there was no other way to rid myself of pain that was too deep to ignore and too vast to escape, I thought death was my only real option. Waking up in the hospital the morning after my failed attempt, however, I awakened with a great feeling of defeat, sadness, and shame. Defeat because I had been unsuccessful in my effort. Sad because I had awakened to find myself still tied to all of the things that had made death a welcomed remedy. With my pain exacerbated by my failure to die, it was now intensified by shame as I struggled to think of an explanation that I could provide the doctors without disclosing my embarrassing secret.

To my great surprise, however, an explanation was not needed. Apparently, I had cried out my pain to the EMTs that had responded to my boyfriend's 911 call for help the night before, and they, in turn, shared that information with the attending emergency room physicians. The doctors who visited my hospital room the following morning already knew my secret and had concluded from my late-night rants that I was in desperate need of psychological help. When they presented that diagnosis to me, however, I was so protective and fearful of my secret that I quickly rejected it and returned home with all my agonies intact.

Two years later, God intensified my woes to a heightened degree by blessing my youngest brother with the NBA opportunity. Being the omniscient Savior that He is, God knew there was no way He could gift Michael with such a life-altering event without my life also being significantly impacted as well. Seeming to care nothing at all about me, or how His decision would further complicate my life, God did as He pleased. Then, He sat back and watched as my life spiraled further out of control.

But was it *really* out of control?

From the human perspective, the answer very much appears to be yes! But the truth of God is that He is *never* without control. And even now as your life reels with afflictions and infractions, God is very much aware of them, and you. In fact, He very well may have ordained your hardships as useful instruments in helping Him shape you into who He has always purposed you to become.

Regardless of what our situations are, God is aware of every ordeal you and I are facing and loves us too much to allow them to just be mundane events with no purpose.

GOD HAS AN APP FOR THAT

A PLETHORA OF TECHNICAL OPTIONS IS easily available to lift us out of a tight spot or distract us in uncomfortable situations. We can glide our fingers over a touch screen and instantly learn how to administer first aid. If we're lonely or upset we can get lost online or in an on-demand movie without leaving the sofa. With all these immediate conveniences, one may wonder if we still need God that much.

The truth is, we need God today just as much as anyone ever did throughout the ages. We may even need Him more. Our culture's ever-evolving technology appears to make us more self-sufficient, more capable, more in control. In reality, these externals can prevent us from relying upon God and abiding in His presence.

The Bible is full of accounts of individuals who trusted God to rescue them from harm or to lend a consoling ear. They earnestly turned to their Deliverer. You can do the same. Through His Word and His presence, God has an app for everything. Just glide your fingers through the pages of the Bible, or even over an e-book reader touch screen, and He'll meet you with fresh courage, strength, and guidance for living life to the fullest. He has the latest technology for meeting your needs today.[5]

—The Authors

...Most of us are too independently minded to naturally embrace the idea of a sovereign God— One who rules over everything He has created, maintaining the absolute right to order His world and to determine our purpose according to a wise, magnificent master design. We may be able to accept this concept in regard to the good things that happen in our lives, but what about the bad things, the inexplicable things, those things for which we cannot see any reason or answers?

The good news is that this is not a "chance world." This is my Father's world! The whole counsel of Scripture leaves us with one inescapable conclusion: heaven rules.

So when everything in your world seems to be giving way and spinning out of control, the fact on which you can stay your heart, mind, and emotions is the reality that God is sovereign, that He is on the throne, and that He has established not only the laws of nature but the duration and outcome of your days.[6]

—Nancy Leigh DeMoss

Who can speak and have it happen if the Lord has not decreed it? Is it not from the mouth of the Most High that both calamities and good things come?
—Lamentations 3:37-38 (NIV)

I create the light and make the darkness. I send good times and bad times. I, the LORD, am the one who does these things.
—Isaiah 45:7 (NIV)

29

He does as he pleases with the powers of heaven and the peoples of the earth. No one can hold back his hand or say to him: "What have you done?"

—Daniel 4:35 (NIV)

In that we are carnal individuals, rarely is it in our nature to immediately think of God or His sovereignty when facing hardships. So having no knowledge or understanding that He was mindful of me, not to mention controlling things around me, I once again became desperate to escape my turmoil. Having cried continuously for weeks to the point of being unable to crawl out of bed to care for my two young children some days, I finally became too emotionally distraught to worry about the "what-ifs" of my familial situation.

You know, the "what-ifs" fears that sometimes take precedence in us when we are seeking other people's approval. Individuals who oftentimes are just as broken as we are but have managed to keep their insecurities in check.

My what-ifs were, what if my family becomes angry with me again because I am unable to hold things together? What if they see me as more of an embarrassment given their newfound notoriety? What if they declare me an unfit parent and try to take my kids from me to try to keep me in line?

Trying desperately not to embrace suicide again, I needed

someone—*anyone*—to tell me how to hold on to my sanity and not to give up on living. Although I had absolutely no idea of what type of help they could offer me, or what that help would require of me, I somehow knew that seeking professional help was what I needed most. Knowing of no other place to turn, I called the emergency room of our local hospital seeking that help.

The woman who answered the phone seemed friendly as she attempted to understand my emergency. Struggling through my steady stream of tears, I tried as best as I could to put my feelings of hopelessness into words. Once realizing the nature of my call, the woman connected me with the psychiatrist on duty, and it was then that I begin to let some of my darkest secrets surface.

Asking me a series of questions to get a better idea of my dilemma, it was when the therapist asked if I felt suicidal that I shamelessly confessed for the first time in my life that suicide was a chronic thought of mine. That it was my attempt to overcome that temptation that had prompted my phone call. Upon hearing that admission, the doctor immediately suggested that I voluntarily commit myself to their depression ward. There, she promised, I would find individuals trained in helping people such as myself.

Even though I had reached out to the emergency room seeking help, I was not at all sure that committing myself to the hospital was the right remedy for me. In that Michael had recently decided to forego his last year of college to enter the NBA draft, he and my parents were receiving statewide media attention like never before. My mother would be incensed if

I did anything to embarrass or bring shame to them, so not wanting to hurt MJ and fearful of creating an issue with my family, I declined the doctor's offer. Confronted with my unwillingness to embrace her suggestion, the doctor informed me that she would nevertheless reserve a hospital room for me, in case I changed my mind.

Hanging up the phone, I once again crumbled into tears as I realized that getting help for all that ailed me would not be easy or without considerable consequences. That *any* help I sought outside of suicide would throw my life into further turmoil and cause enormous conflicts within my family. And having failed at suicide previously, I feared failing again and having to endure even more shame. So for a while, I just surrendered to my tears. As nightfall came, however, so did my fears of the recurring nightmares of my father doing and whispering things to me that no father should ever do or whisper to his child—to anyone's child!

With those debilitating memories crippling me mentally, I became so desperate for peace that I stepped beyond fears of my parent's wrath and headed to the hospital. Consumed with a desire to beat the wars that were waging in my head, I needed someone, *anyone*, to help me fight them. And having sought help from my parents previously at the suggestions of a friend only for my mother to ask me to leave their home, I knew of no other place to turn but to the emergency room.

If someone had told me back then that one day I would look upon my time spent on what many in our small town called the "crazy" floor with great appreciation, I would have brushed off such claims as foolish. Today however, I dare not box God in or downplay how far He will allow us to travel in order to equip us for the purpose for which He gave us life.

Brief and in no way curing me of all that afflicted me, my stay in the hospital granted me the opportunity to come face to face with other individuals struggling with some of my issues.

For the first time in my life, I met people like me who had been violated, was frightened, confused, and mentally overwhelmed by their experiences. Until attending the mandated group therapy sessions and hearing some of their stories, I had always assumed that sexual abuse was something that had happened only to me. The fact that gaining my newfound knowledge required me to be *barred-in* nightly on the seventh floor with individuals who were, in some cases, far more mentally challenged than me did not lessen my appreciation for having come to learn that I was not alone in my experience or feelings of hopelessness. And although I missed my children, I knew that I was no good for them.

How could I be? I was not even good for me!

The solitude that I found in the hospital was short-lived, however. My family reacted to my hospitalization with considerable protest, and pressure for me to leave came from every direction. And while I had prepared for my parents' opposition by asking the therapist to restrict their accessibility to me, I had not considered how other family members would react.

But react, they did!

Of everyone's outcry, however, it was my grandparents' reaction that distressed me the most. Deciding that my wellness was not worth their sorrow, I checked out of the hospital against doctors' wishes and returned home with all of my afflictions intact. But despite my brief hospital stay and its abrupt ending, I came away from my time there with a clear understanding that there were (are) an abundance of people in the world like me. People in need of learning that they are not alone in their suffering and who can find comfort in knowing that others can relate to their pain. Especially when it seems that God is not mindful of their despair.

FROM THE PLACE OF EMPTINESS

THERE WILL BE TIMES IN LIFE when nothing makes any sense. All is dark. Confusion reigns. We hoped for something great and came up empty. There we stand with nothing in our hands—no plans, no dreams, no hopes—nothing but desolation.

But be assured that even in this place of darkness, God is present. This can be the prologue to a great story. This can be the backdrop to a great adventure. Throughout history, every great work of God started in this exact place of emptiness. This is the kind of situation that causes Him to roll up His sleeves and rub His hands together in anticipation.

God gives shape to those things that do not yet have any form. Just as Michelangelo "saw" the sculpture inside the stone, so also God sees what we cannot see. What is now hidden from our sight will someday be revealed. God fills those things that are empty. His light easily overcomes the darkness in our lives. When Jesus enters the place of darkness, it will never be the same. Laughter will return. What is dead will be brought to life.

Here in this unlikely place, God's Spirit is hovering, waiting, ready to do the impossible.[7]

—The Authors

Many years later, I founded my nonprofit organization, Let's Start A Conversation (LSAC), based solely on my hospital experience. Mindful that we all need to be encouraged from time to time, LSAC is my way of bringing individuals together to engage in conversations of hope without requiring them to submit themselves to mental wards to discover that they are not alone in their brokenness. LSAC is not, however, an organization with a mission to replace psychiatric wards or downplay the need for counseling. It is just my way of paying my gratitude forward by being a tangible voice of encouragement to those in need of such.

Is it not the potter's right to use *any* tool He chooses, to mold us into the person He created us to be? Even now, as you are grappling with situations that seem to be overwhelming you, God is not trying to destroy you. He is just using your pain to shape you into the beautiful vessel He always purposed you to be.

Does a clay pot argue with its maker? Does the clay dispute with the one who shapes it, saying, "Stop, you're doing it wrong!"
—Isaiah 45:9 (NLT)

BY DESIGN

Thank you for making me so wonderfully complex! Your workmanship is marvelous—how well I know it.
Psalm 139:14 NLT

HAVE YOU EVER SET BENEATH A TREE in the summer and looked up? Think about the intricacy of the leaves, how they connect to the tree. Consider the texture in the bark, and picture the way the sun shines on the veins of the leaf. You can almost hear the sap flowing.

It's an easy conclusion to think that only God could make something like that. Something so marvelously complex. Each part fits together into a beautiful whole. The tree has its place in the landscape. Even in the wild it towers majestically above the earth.

When it comes to thinking about yourself, do you see yourself as made by the same hand? The One who made the trees made you. If you admire the workmanship of the tree, you can also appreciate His artistry in you. You are marvelously complex. All your parts fit together into a beautiful whole.

You're much more intricate than a tree, but the One who lovingly made nature also made you. You can rest in the wonder of His artwork. If God put all that energy into something that cannot even talk, He surely put even more creative zeal into you. In this moment, revel in the wonder of God's workmanship—you.[8]

—The Authors

CHAPTER THREE
Challenged To Change

Many of the nonprofits that exist today resulted from someone's effort to do something positive with devastating events that shook the core of their existence and, in many cases, propelled them towards the very purpose for which God had created them. Purpose-filled events that they stumbled upon as they fought their way through tunnels of darkness and excruciating pain. We need only to look at the life of Candace Lightner to see how true that statement is.

Candace was a grief-stricken mother faced with the death of her thirteen-year-old daughter, Cari, due to the actions of a drunk driver. It was that painful loss that became the catalyst for her establishing Mothers Against Drunk Driving (MADD), through which she not only endeavored to spare other parents her heartache, but she also spearheaded legislation that criminalized drunk driving throughout the country.

Could God have prevented the death of her young daughter?

Absolutely!

But what God knew that Cari's parents could have never known at the onset of their ordeal, however, were all the lives that would be impacted by their loss, strength, and courage. Having had a plan for Candace long before He gave her three children that would each have a collision with a driver under the influence, God knew that He would one day use her and her voice in ways that differed and far exceeded any expectations or aspirations she had of her own. Her loss, pain, and willingness to use her voice to spare us similar experiences, will forever be a medium through which we all have benefited.

As preposterous as it might seem at times, if we are to thrive as a society, it is imperative that we all become more concerned with each other's healthiness, especially our mental and emotional well-being. While our physical afflictions indeed impact the lives of those with whom we are most intimately connected, our mental and emotional unhealthiness often extends beyond those relationships, with devastating and far-reaching consequences. The barrage of mass shootings in recent years illustrates that truth overwhelmingly, as thousands of families have been destroyed by assailants unknown to them, with the trajectory of cultures forever changed.

The fact that I attempted suicide and you are contemplating it, not to mention the thousands of others who succeeded in their effort, speaks to how crucial it is that we become more attentive to our own and each other's mental wellness. Personally, I would love to see more of us affirming each other rather than ridiculing each other. And because I believe that you deserve the chance to feel better about you and your life, I am willing to do my part by sharing my experiences with you; good and bad. Hoping very much that something I share with you here will help you strive for your future.

Regardless of how much I want that for you, however, you must want it too and begin fighting vigorously for it. And while I know that it is not as easy as flipping a switch, it is as easy as reaching out to mental-health-focused entities that will walk with you through your dark moments. Organizations comprised of individuals that do not want to shame you, judge you, or harm you, but will help you find the resources you need. And as much as you may yearn for that help to come from family and friends, please know that they may not be equipped to help you. So, please don't be upset with them if they can't or won't!

As someone who continues to embrace the services of a therapist, I have come to understand that I am worth the effort of reaching beyond anyone that hinders my wellness, to enlist the help of skilled individuals familiar with afflictions such as mine. You owe yourself nothing less!

SWITCHING THE PRICE TAG

PART OF THE TWISTED THINKING of the fallen human condition is a tendency to switch the price tag on God's creation—to devalue human life while elevating the importance of other created things. We can sometimes be more concerned about the condition of our pets and our flower beds, for example, than about the people with whom God has chosen to populate our lives. For while each of these individual specimens of His creation is certainly important to Him—important enough that He feeds the "birds of the air" and adorns the "lilies of the field" (Matt. 6:26, 28)—His uncommon care for mankind goes beyond all other loves.

Even in the act of creation itself, we see God speaking many things into existence—trees, plants, animals, fish, the moon, sun, and stars. But when creating human life, it was as though He rolled up His sleeves and got His hands involved, forming man "from the dust of the ground" (Gen. 2:7), then fashioning woman from a rib taken out of the man's side (verses 21-22).

This is why we are not surprised when we later see the tender, caring heart of Jesus reaching out to the poor, the weak, the oppressed, and disenfranchised— dirtying His hands over people many would consider of far less value than the other "things" in their lives.

We know from observing our God in Scripture that every life is precious to Him, to be treated with great care, affection, and compassion. May our affections and actions be shaped by priorities that matter most to Him.[9]

—Nancy Leigh DeMoss

What is man that you are mindful of him, and the son of man that you care for him? Yet you have made him a little lower than the heavenly beings and crowned him with glory and honor.
—Psalm 8:4-5 (ESV)

As a society that loves challenges—ice-bucket, marathons, the polar bear, and the like—what would we be like as a community if we challenged each other to become voices of encouragement to each other?

What if you were to embrace my efforts to encourage you, took life-sustaining actions to heal your brokenness, and then used your voice to speak words of encouragement to those that you encounter throughout your day?

What if you then challenged those you encouraged to duplicate your efforts within their families and community?

Can you imagine the phenomenal impact it would have on our world as a whole?

Then let's do something constructive with your pain other than contemplate suicide. Join me in using our experiences with brokenness to help nurture someone else through theirs.

Who better to do such things than you and me, given that we understand how it feels to be desperate, despondent, and hopeless? After all, it is those same feelings that have connected us.

Could it be that collaborating for the good that our pain can do is the very reason God allowed us to have this moment together?

Could it be that He wanted us to combine our voices and become vessels of encouragement to each other and then to others?

As you give thought to how your life could impact our world for good, it is my sincere hope that you come to view your hardships from a new perspective. Doing so will help you change the narratives regarding them.

CONSOLED TO CONSOLE

All praise to the God and Father...God of all healing counsel! He comes alongside us when we go through hard times, and...he brings us alongside someone else.
—2 Corinthians 1:3-4 MSG

"IT TAKES ONE TO KNOW ONE"—The old adage we associate with the identification of character hold true for empathy in suffering as well. You can't understand the grief of a widow until you've suffered the loss of a spouse. You can't grasp the pain of being terminated from your job until you've been fired. You really won't be able to empathize with the fear and dread of terminal cancer unless you have been diagnosed with it.

But when you have suffered—really suffered—you gain the capacity to be a true source of understanding to those who are currently suffering. You are now equipped to become one of God's greatest resources for those who are in distress, sharing the comfort and consolation you have received from your times alone with Him.

Anyone can be empathetic toward people who are hurting, but not just anyone can walk with another through their pain. Take notice of people in distress and ask God whether you are the one through whom He might bring consolation. If you are willing to be His partner, God can use you to make the world a little less painful for those whose lives you touch.[10]

—The Authors

Honestly, I don't know if I would be so committed to encouraging you had I not once been in great need of it myself. With so many individuals possessing a hardened heart towards hurting and afflicted people today and social media making it easier than ever to discredit, dismiss, and ridicule each other, would I have been indifferent too, if not for my own life experiences?

Would I have merely looked upon the spirit of hopelessness that is permeating throughout our world, shed a tear or two, then moved on with my life without giving any real thought to global afflictions?

Maybe!

Probably!

It is painful to admit that but no less true. Depression, illness, unemployment, drugs, violence, and a host of other similar heartrending circumstances surround us daily. Rarely do we stop to really consider the depth of their devastation, however, until it is our life that is being adversely affected by them.

It is when "*them*" has transitioned to *me* or *us* that our hearts soften and our minds begin to grasp the realness of the menacing situations. Even then, however, many of us often fail to recognize that it is God who has allowed our discomfort for a purpose that we can never truly understand until we tune in to Him and permit Him to reveal it to us.

WHEN YOUR SPIRIT GROWS FAINT within you, it is I who know your way. This is one of the benefits of weakness. It highlights the fact that you cannot find your way without help from Me. If you are feeling weary or confused, you can choose to look away from those feelings and turn wholeheartedly toward Me. Pour out your heart freely, and then rest in the Presence of the One who *knows your way* perfectlyall the way to heaven.

Continue this practice of gazing at Me even during the times when you're feeling strong and confident. In fact, this is when you are most at risk of going the wrong direction. Instead of assuming that you know the next step of your journey, train yourself to make your plans in My Presence—asking Me to guide you. Remember that *My ways and thoughts are higher than yours, as the heavens are higher than the earth.* Let this remembrance draw you into worshiping Me, *the High and Lofty One who inhabits eternity* and who reaches down to help you.[11]

—Sarah Young

LEVERAGE

A SEEMINGLY TRIFLING INCIDENT CAN CHANGE a life. Walking off a troopship, a young soldier was singled out at random for an assignment. He stepped away from his companions and never saw them again. Every one of his shipmates was killed: he alone returned home alive.

You never know what you have in your hands. David had a stone, but it toppled the monster Goliath and stopped evil plans to enslave a nation. A young boy had a lunch bag with some bread and fish in it. But, in the hands of Jesus, that lunch fed five thousand.

Small things can make a big difference. Self-defense experts call this principle leverage. With the right leverage, a small person can deflect an attack from a much larger person. A slight turn of the wrist, a pivot at the waist and a dangerous attacker is tossed harmlessly aside.

What can God do with what you have in your hands? The bits and pieces of your life may appear mundane, but in God's hands, they are tools that can change eternity. Offer your words, your work, whatever you have in front of you to Him, and see what miracle He will do.[12]

—The Authors

CHAPTER FOUR

Shhh—Take It All In

The pendulum of life is forever swinging and as individuals struggling to live in an imperfect world, we sway with it. Some days, we embrace our life with dreams and whims as we strategically map out our future with eager anticipation. Other days, the prospect of even having a future seems dim and far-fetched as we struggle just to make it through another chaotic pain-riddled day.

For some of us, getting past dark moments in our lives will forever be our greatest challenge. Failure to triumph over them, however, is sure to deprive us of a future filled with incredible possibilities enfolded within it. Possibilities that are often inconceivable to us when clouded by our difficult moments.

The World Health Organization's published suicide statistics highlight the fact that not all of us are winning the fight against the temptation to quit life. Daily, thousands of individuals throughout the world intentionally embrace suicide as the remedy for their broken spirit, or unwittingly succumb to it due to drug overdose. But whether intentional or accidental, individuals in both scenarios sought to escape painful moments by embracing remedies that ultimately denied them the opportunity of learning that pain does not last always.

It is true that when our life has been scarred by painful events, the memories of our heart-breaching experiences will remain with us forever. But what we often fail to realize during those times, however, is the fact that God really can deliver us from the agony of those experiences if we allow Him too. In some cases, it is just a matter of being granted the time to work through the pain as we are taught the depth of our inner strength. Had God not ignored my pleas for death and brought me back from the brink of it, my name would have also been added to the ever-growing list of individuals who regarded suicide as the only feasible solution for situations that, at the time, seemed insurmountable to overcome.

When I embraced suicide for the third and final time in 1991, I did so genuinely believing that I had learned from my earlier failures and had finally figured out how to succeed at it. What I did not know, however, was the unapologetic declaration that God makes to all of us in James 4:15b (NIV, emphasis added):

*"If it is the Lord's will, we **will** live."*

Today, many years later, I now understand that it is never God's desire for anyone to commit suicide. The fact that some are successful in their effort while others are not should never be interpreted as God agreeing with the decision. It is far more likely that those who succeeded failed to heed the warnings that God gives to us all.

You know, those intuitive inclinations that tell us that the path we are traveling is dangerous. That we should turn back and go another way. Those big, and sometimes small, cautionary signs that we sometimes choose audaciously to ignore.

Hard-headed, strong-willed, defiant, or just plain immature, I was guilty of such a mindset and refused to accept my previous suicidal failures as deterrents. Believing instead, that I had figured out a fail-proof system, I strategically and methodically planned my date with death like I had never done before. Then one July morning, with my plan solidified in my heart, I awakened and began to put that plan in motion.

With my children, ages 12 and 14 at the time in North Carolina with family, I was comforted by the fact that they would not be immediately impacted by my decision. Many years later, I came to realize just how selfish I had been towards them, however.

There is no way you nor I can commit suicide and not impact those we love in a profound, life-altering way that will remain with them for the remainder of their life. And whether we intend to or not, when we as parents embrace suicide, we are inadvertently influencing our children with the unverbalized, yet implied belief that we found life too strenuous to endure and chances are that they may find it to be as well. And if such is the case, suicide is an acceptable solution.

Given that the very nature of their young lives and personal growth will consist of peaks and valleys that will indeed include intervals of difficulties and pain, do we really want to offer up suicide to them as a viable solution?

More than anything we say, it is our actions that will influence our children the most. I will forever regret the role I played by implying to my children, and anyone else, that suicide is ever an appropriate remedy for pain. In that I am so grateful to be alive today, many years later, clearly it is not!

During my heart-ravaging days of yesteryear, however, I was so demoralized by my life that I could not see beyond my anguish. And like more people today than ever before, I embraced a resolution that appeared best and most logical at the time. And even if it was not the better of my options, it unquestionably was the easiest.

Or so I thought!

On that fateful July morning, having decided that I had endured as much of my life as I could stand to bear, I kissed my husband goodbye as he headed off to work. Then I turned my attention to the to-do-list I had compiled days earlier, consisting of chores that I wanted to complete before taking my last breath with achieving death the final task on that list.

Cleaning my home as close to spotless as I possibly could, I vacuumed, mopped, and did every other household chore that I thought needed to be completed to illustrate to all who visited my home upon learning of my death that I was a tidy person.

Shhh, not a word!

Yes, I realize now how vain and absurd it was of me to

care more about people judging my housekeeping skills than my injurious actions. But such concerns originated from my childhood and followed me into adulthood.

Surely I am not the only one who was taught to "never leave your home untidy because there is no guarantee that you will return to it. You never want people to visit it and judge you by its uncleanliness." As well as, "always make sure you have on clean underwear before you leave home, just in case you end up in the hospital. You never want people there to think that you are unclean." So after cleaning my home as close to perfection as I could get it, I proceeded to do nothing less with my body.

Isn't it funny how such childhood lessons remain with us even when plotting our death? At the time, it never occurred to me that I could have ignored both admonishments. The fact that I was contemplating suicide, however, speaks to my diminished ability to rationalize proficiently. The propensity to embrace suicide happens most often when we are entrenched in the throes of a situation that has been magnified to a heightened degree and cloaked in a false belief that there is no logical way to escape it other than taking our life. Trapped in what seemed like a continuous rollercoaster of mayhem, I was desperate for the turbulence in my life to end, and killing myself seemed to be the most feasible solution at that time.

Have you ever ended up at a party that you did not even know you would be attending until you arrived?

Imagine arriving and instantly realizing how ill-prepared you are for the festivities. A surreal and unfamiliar environment that immediately made you feel out of place, uncomfortable, and ill-equipped. Infringed upon in ways you never anticipated, soon your most overwhelming desire is to flee the scene. But having been dragged to the party by those you love, you know that you are not in the driver seat. At their mercy and wanting very much to please them even if it hurts you, you resign yourself to just trailing behind them hoping for the best.

Once firmly deposited inside the gala, you watch from afar as your loved ones mingle and make themselves comfortable in their new surroundings. Beleaguered with unresolved family woes, personal insecurities and feelings of inadequacies, you just hide out in the corner trying hard not to get in anyone's way. And when the soiree grows to unfathomable dimensions, with things being said and asked of you that distorts reality, you find yourself saturated with such an onslaught of new dysfunctions that you just want to flee them all. And for the sake of those who assume that having an abundance of possessions or certain people in one's life will resolve all that ails you, let me take this moment to denounce that belief as I describe the depth of *my* mental unhealthiness.

I was chasing death even though I was physically healthy with two beautiful children and a husband that I loved. I owned my own home, had thousands of dollars in my bank account, and a boatload of new experiences as a result of my brother's superstardom. In terms of worldly *goodness*, I had more than I had ever had, yet none of it freed me from my pursuit of death.

Honestly, it was the fear of losing the affection of people that I loved, my yearning for their approval, fear of being ostracized by them, and the fear of losing my possessions that largely contributed to my pain. Though, as you have learned from my earlier disclosures, I already had self-worth deficiencies. All of these later concerns just added layers to those.

But I do not share any of this with you seeking your sympathy. I share it with you because daily, many of you crawl out of our beds after a restless night of sleep and rush out into the world fervently pursuing self-indulging titles, other people's accolades, and a surplus of possessions hoping that accumulating them will somehow cure the emptiness deep within you.

With the aid of television and social media, you observe other people's lives from afar, craving the labels they wear, the lifestyle they portray, and a host of other things they own while having no clue whatsoever of the cost. Nor do you know their daily struggle to maintain them all. Yet, as members of an idolatry-ladened culture, you covet their life while discrediting your own as if it has no value.

Please hear me, accumulating an abundance of possessions or having specific people in our life does not cure us, nor in the end, fulfill the purpose for which God gave us life. As you will come to learn in a later YASTYS series of sharing, I lost all of my *stuff,* including my home, and came to learn a lesson that I am not sure I could have learned any other way.

FINDING CONTENTMENT

IN A CULTURE THAT CONTINUALLY PROMOTES the idea that more is better, finding contentment feels like an uphill battle. There's always something that lures you into thinking that if you only had that, if you could only go there, if you could just live the way they do, then you'd be satisfied.

But people who have found true contentment know that acquiring "more" never satisfies. True contentment comes when you realize that in your life with God, you already have everything you'll ever need and then some. Becoming content with your life isn't an impossible goal to strive for; it's a reality that's available to you now.

Gratitude for what God has already given you is an essential element to learning to be content. Thank God for His provision, and rest in the knowledge that He will continue to provide. Ask Him to make you more aware each day of the abundance you already have, appreciating how little it takes to lead a truly satisfied life.

When you view your possessions—and your desire for more—from God's perspective, you will also begin to identify those things in your life that have eternal value—and you'll discover that that is where true contentment lies.[13]

—The Authors

On that fateful July afternoon, when my mental anguish tormented me to the edge of life, I no longer had the strength to fight off my yearning for death. And with no support system in place that allowed my pain to surface or to help me work through it, I ran towards death with a determination and desperation to finally succeed in my efforts. And although I had gone to church all my life and knew *of* God, I did not genuinely know Him. Nor give Him much thought at all back then.

Never viewing Him as being a viable answer for any of what was ailing me, I never thought to pray to Him for peace of mind. Or bothered to ask Him to comfort me through all the things that were making my life so burdensome and unbearable. And, as I stated earlier, I gave no thought to the detrimental impact that taking my life would have on my children beyond believing that they would be better off without me. So, surrendering to that belief, among others, I checked off all the things on my to-do-list that summer day, and then I went throughout my home collecting every pill I could find to ingest: prescribed and otherwise.

Having embraced overdosing as my preferred method of death at the onset of my suicidal journey, I theorized after my overdose failure that I had failed because I had not taken enough pills. Determined not to duplicate that mistake this time around, I not only ingested every kind of pill I could find, but I also washed them all down with an entire fifth of Bourbon.

Pursuing death as vigorously as I could, I hoped that if I were unsuccessful in my efforts, I would at the very least end up comatose like Karen Quinlan. A young woman whose ingestion of a mixture of pills and booze resulted in her being in a coma for 10 years before finally succumbing to death. Fanatically seeking an escape, I was willing to settle for a coma if it would render me numb and unconscious.

So as the world outside my home buzzed with life, I ingested the deadly concoction, crawled on my bed, and waited for death to come. But it would be the events that followed those actions that illuminated the preeminence of God and solidified forever, my utter understanding that it is He alone who decides who lives and who dies.

"I am the one who kills and gives life; I am the one who wounds and heals; no one can be rescued from my powerful hand," declares God in Deuteronomy 32:39b (NLT).

Even with the most horrific events, it is He who decides!

One person stumbles, falls, hits their head and dies—another person gets shot in the head and lives to talk about it. One person loses control of their vehicle, strikes a tree, and succumbs to death—another person gets in an automobile accident so horrific that their vehicle is unrecognizable, and walks away without a scratch. One person is sickened with the Coronavirus and dies—another person is sickened with it and recovers. Try as we might to analyze these events, there is no absolute logic that we can apply to them beyond the fact that God alone holds our life in His hands.

Without giving *any* thought to God deciding whether I lived or died, I strategized, did household chores, showered, and then crawled on my bed to await death. But not even our best-laid plans are a match for God's, however!

As I laid on my bed with my bedroom walls spinning me into oblivion, fading but not yet fully submerged in unconsciousness, the phone on my nightstand rang and I instinctively reached out to answer it, falling off my bed in the process. Even now, as I recall the sequence of events that followed that phone call, I do so shaking my head and shuddering. Now, I am so very cognizant of just how different my life and the lives of my children would have been if that phone not rang. Or, had silly old me not bothered to answer it—the endless list of experiences and moments with them that I am grateful for today, that were so inconceivable to me back then.

Nothing in my life at that time gave any hint that peace and joy could, or would, be part of my story one day. So when I reached for the phone, I was not at all trying to save my life. I merely answered it because answering ringing phones was a natural reaction in those days. Today, however, I can sit next to my phone and ignore its rings with ease, thanks largely to the asinine number of telemarketing calls I receive daily.

As God would have it to be on that fateful July day, however, I picked up the phone and found my friend Michelle on the other end. With it having become our custom over the years, to check on each other from time to time, she had chosen this most inopportune time to check on me. She would tell me later, after our ordeal was over, that it had not been her intent to phone me at all on that particular day. But, for reasons that she could not explain, she was suddenly overcome with such an urgency to talk to me that she had stopped in the midst of her chores to call me.

Noting my slurred speech at the onset of the call, she had initially assumed that she had interrupted my afternoon nap. As I faded in and out of our conversation, she merely concluded that I was still quite sleepy but was politely enduring her chatter rather than tell her to call me back later. And when I finally stopped contributing to the conversation altogether, she hung up believing that I had simply fallen back to sleep. But as she returned to her chores, she was overcome with such an alarming feeling of anxiety that she decided to put her chores on hold and come check on me.

Arriving at my home a little while later, she was elated to see my car there. Embracing its presence as a sign that I was still at home, she was glad to learn that her trip would not be a wasted one. And with that belief at the forefront of her mind, she stepped to my front door and proceeded to ring my doorbell. When her efforts failed to bring me to the door, she immediately wondered if the doorbell was working properly.

Listening more intently for its chime than before, she rang the bell again and soon noted that it was indeed working properly, so when it still went unanswered, she began to knock loudly on the door. And when her banging still did not bring me to the door, she tested the doorknob to see if by chance it was unlocked.

It was not!

Once she had exhausted all of her available options for the front door, she moved to the side door and proceeded to repeat them.

Still nothing!

Realizing that her efforts should have produced a response, she wondered if my husband Rick had returned home during

60

the time it had taken her to travel across town on the bus and had taken me with him. In that cell phones were not as prevalent then as they are now, however, she had no way to call him to inquire. With all of her options exhausted and left only to mull over our earlier phone exchange, she began to wonder if maybe there had been more to my slurred speech and sleepiness than just an afternoon nap.

Alarmed now by her unsettling thoughts, she began to move feverishly from door to door, banging and ringing doorbells. Nothing she did, however, yielded different results.

Forced to give up, she pushed aside her frantic fears by consoling herself with the notion that I indeed was not home. Making herself a mental note to phone me later to let me know that she had stopped by, she left and headed back to the bus stop. Upon arriving there, however, she was again overcome with such feelings of anxiousness that she turned on her heels and began walking the couple of blocks back to my home. Once again at my front door, she began ringing my doorbell more franticly than before. When her rings still went unanswered, she grabbed the doorknob mechanically, not really expecting any different results from those that she had gotten earlier. To her amazement, however, the door opened!

Quickly stepping inside, she raced to my bedroom and there she found me straddling death. And after summoning the help that we both needed, we each were blessed to walk away from the surreal experience with a testimony that defies logic but testifies to God's saving grace. Appreciating that grace, however, was not my immediate reaction. That appreciation would come later—many years later, to be exact! My initial reaction upon waking and finding myself still among the living and still tied to my life was tremendous anger.

Not with Michelle, but definitely with God!

Isn't it funny how I was so quick to blame Him for being powerful enough to thwart my suicidal efforts but had not viewed Him previously as being powerful enough to rescue me from all the things that were making suicide such an attractive option?

Honestly, I never thought He cared about me and up to this point, nothing in my life led me to think otherwise. Seemingly indifferent to my afflictions, He seemed to only show up in my life in ways that heightened my distress and made it more difficult.

Or, so I deemed!

FRAGILE, BUT LOVED

THINK FOR A MOMENT about how fragile we are. To stay alive, we need the perfect combination of oxygen and nitrogen in the air we breathe, just the right amount of water and other chemicals in our bodies, a steady supply of the right proteins and other nutrients to sustain us. Dangers abound. Mishaps and microbes threaten us. Bombs and bacteria can kill us.

Why would God design us humans to be so… breakable? Does He delight in dangling us over danger? After shaping stars and building continents, did He run out of durable building supplies when He fashioned us from the dust? Doesn't He realize that it can be really scary sometimes to be human?

Maybe God does understand our fears. Maybe He knows even better than we do how susceptible we are to harm. But when our backs are up against the wall, does that mean God is also cornered?

Absolutely not! God never runs out of options, and every one of our vulnerabilities is an opportunity for Him to express His creative love for us.

Ask Him for what you need. He is always listening. His solution may not be what you imagined, but it will always be more than enough.[14]

—The Authors

As I laid in the hospital, coughing up the charcoal the doctors had used to neutralize my pill concoction, I seethed with anger. And even more so when a local politician died a few days later while campaigning.

It made absolutely no sense to me that God would take a man who wanted to live, yet leave me behind even though I had far less to offer the world and did not want to be here.

It also seemed absolutely ludicrous and confounding to me that God would decide to open my front door at that exact moment in my life but had not bothered to open it all the times my family and I had been locked out because of the door's automatic lock.

Where was He during those times?

That door had been an object of contention between Rick and me for several years. In place when we purchased the home, it irked me profusely that he never found the time to replace it even though renovating homes was his profession. On more occasions than I care to count, the kids and I had been locked out because of it. So much so that we all came to learn not to venture out of it without our keys or leaving it ajar.

Despite my anger, however, I knew that the locked door did not become unlocked on its own. Accepting that fact meant that I could not ignore the indisputable truth that God was mindful of me and had purposely spared my life. From steering Michelle's actions to reviving me from the deadly concoction I had ingested, He had interrupted my plans with plans of His own. Then graciously and mercifully, He allowed me to recover from the ordeal without suffering any adverse effects from my actions.

Baffled by all that He had done, I became curious to learn what God saw in me that I did not see in myself, and I challenged Him to show it to me. *"If you won't let me die, Lord, then show me how to live this life you have given me,"* I pleaded.

Thankfully, He did just that!

THE FINGERPRINTS OF GOD

HOW DO YOU TELL THE DIFFERENCE between the work of God and mere human effort? For those of us who live in cold climates, we know what it means to wrestle with snow. A heavy snowfall can cripple a city, and it can take hours or even days to dig ourselves out. We get up, walk outside, and hear the sounds of shovels scraping the sidewalks, snowplows grinding over asphalt, and snow blowers roaring as they throw snow into great piles on either side of the driveway. Yet, when it thaws, God effortlessly and silently removes the snow without any huffing or puffing.

In the same way, the work of God seldom attracts a lot of attention. Typically, it isn't noisy or flashy. Most of the time, the work of God comes in the form of quiet miracles, gentle transformations, invisible works of wonder. But the results are lasting change. The great enterprises of men rise and fall, then they fade from our memory. But the fingerprints of God are on the eternal. The work He does through His children is inspired as they spend time alone with Him and then go out to touch the world.[15]

—The Authors

As much as I want you to tune in to your ability to live a joy-filled life too, I dare not lie to you by proclaiming that my progression forward happened overnight or pain-free. Many days the ugliness of my life continued to overwhelm me. But once I wholly surrendered to the task of living out my story regardless of its challenges, I no longer tried to do it alone. Instead, I focused intently on God, trusting Him to show me what He saw in me.

Who else can show us our worth to Him but Him?

Plus, have you ever noticed how ten people can see the same incident and all have different versions and perspectives? No longer desiring to see me through anyone's eyes but His, I wanted to get to know the person for whom He had stayed the hand of death. And, I wanted to know *why* He did it!

Man, the road God had me travel to learn who I was in His eyes was brutal, to say the least, but also very liberating!

Making me confront layers of self-pity, He also challenged me with the task of learning how to rebuke vilifying, self-loathing messages instilled in me by childhood experiences and nurtured by adulthood coping mechanisms. Teaching me that I was not alone regardless of what the little voices in my head proclaimed, He then helped me replace my sorrowful *"I can't"* cries of defeat with courageous *"If you say I can Lord, then I can"* declarations of strength as He stripped away the shame and guilt that had long taken up residence in me.

Laboring me with the grueling task of learning to like myself, which is far harder than learning to like other people I think, God infused me with the courage to hold my head up and say publicly all the things that my family would not allow me to discuss with them privately. Thus freeing me of the burden of *pretending* that all was well so that I could learn to live an authentic life of wellness, which aided me in rejecting luring and lurking thoughts of suicide.

Given that my mental healthiness did not happen instantaneously or without considerable effort, chances are yours will not either. Indubitably, you will have to make a definitive decision that *you* are worth the most daunting work that you will probably ever do. Then, you will have to commit yourself to the task regardless of how taxing it may be.

Many days, your most significant work will consist vastly of convincing yourself that you have the right to enjoy your day. That it is indeed God's desire for you to have joy-filled days.

I have come to learn personally that my joy is not tied to people, places, or things. While such entities contribute significantly to my happiness, my *joy* centers solely on God and my peace of mind. To sustain serenity in my life, I make every effort to indulge in conversations, embrace activities, and socially interact with people that enhance my well-being rather than disrupt it, whenever possible.

Protective of my mental healthiness now more than ever before, I tend to find joy in some of the simplest things. Things that I never really took the time to embrace or appreciate previously.

Things like walking alone in my favorite park, tuning into the wonders of God—the soft breeze on my face; the landscape of greenery or lack thereof; the setting of an orange sun; the refreshing tickle of misting rain; the nibbling squirrel or gazing deer that stop momentarily to observe me—All awe-inspiring creations that remind me of God's awesomeness. Not one of them created outside of His plan!

Now find comfort, strength, and hope in the fact that as He was with them, He was no less deliberate in creating you!

GOD'S ARTISTRY

GOD'S ARTISTRY IS EVERYWHERE. THE MOON reflected in the quiet waters of a lake in the woods, the unrestrained laughter of a child, a bride adorned on her wedding day, a song rising up from a grateful heart, an elderly couple walking hand in hand.

Beauty invites us to celebrate God's goodness in our lives. It catches our attention; it causes us to pause and consider. It elevates us as human beings. It inspires us to care about things that matter. That's why God's fingerprints are found in each of us—not just physical attractiveness, but beautiful thoughts, stories, attitudes, and relationships. All of this points heavenward.

By itself this artistry can be a pathway into the presence of God. Vibrant rainbows and warm smiles, kind words, and soothing voices—these are all gifts from God, calling us to Him, reminding us that

He isn't finished with us yet. We are each a work in progress. The full wonder of what He is doing in us has not yet been revealed. Something better lies ahead. We are each a masterpiece created by God. The more we linger in His transforming presence, the more His beauty is reflected in our lives.[16]

—The Authors

Let's make a collaborative and conscientious agreement that regardless of fears that try to entice us to dwell in the dark moments of our lives by doubting our worth, we will strive to remind each other that we are God's magnificent wonders too. Let's remind each other to continually tune into God, granting Him the opportunity to show us just who He had in mind when He created us.

It's not too late!

Tune out and move away from anyone and *every*one that makes you think otherwise. And since you are already standing on the edge of your life contemplating suicide, what do you have to lose? If you turn to God and later decide that He is not powerful enough to deliver you from your pain, the option of suicide will still be there waiting to welcome you back. But right now, you owe yourself the opportunity to see what unrealized wonders awaits you on the other side of your pain.

FRESH STRENGTH

Those who trust in the Lord will find new strength.... They will run and not grow weary. They will walk and not faint.
—Isaiah 40:31 (NLT)

ON THE SOCCER FIELD, THE LOP-SIDED loss tastes bitter to the six-year-old. He didn't mean to score one for the other team. Dejected by the final outcome and by his own performance, the boy trudges off the field. But suddenly, he spots his dad waiting at the edge of the field. The father gently reaches for his son's hand. Hope quietly resurges in the youngster as he clenches his father's sure grip.

Your heavenly Father is reaching for your hand too. He knows you work hard. He knows you give your all but sometimes come up short. He knows when you're worn out by life and feel faint in your faith. God understands when you feel like crawling into a hole or plopping down in defeat. When you feel like you've endured one too many lop-sided losses, God wants you to simply put your hand in His—and trust. He promises to exchange His strength for your weariness.

So what are you holding on to these days? Are your fingers wrapped around your relationships, your work, your social calendar? What or whom are you trusting in for hope, renewal, and vitality? Put your trust in the One who longs to revive you with fresh strength.[17]

—The Authors

CHAPTER FIVE

Mocked But Healing

"This sounds like a happy-go-lucky woman everyone would want to spend time with. If she has to write a book, obviously Michael hasn't given her enough of his money. (Sorry, just being catty)" wrote Ms. Winters, a radio personality in Chicago who mocked me to a colleague upon receiving a media blast about an upcoming book signing in her area for my first book.

In her email banter with her colleague, Ms. Winters inadvertently included my email and the statement above landed in my inbox. Disappointed, but not surprised by her mocking, given that Barbara Walters had slandered me even more vilely on ABC's 20/20, I immediately responded with a message of my own,

"Ms. Winters, could it just be that I have something worthy to say and not even Michael's money lessens the necessity of doing that? Oh, but then that would mean that we don't live in a society with people who measure other people's contributions by the amount of money attached to it. It very well could be that you would be greatly helped by reading my book. In it, I talk honestly about our need of learning to love each other unconditionally, without materialism being the measuring stick.

I am proud today to be able to look beyond my past for the pain it inflicted upon me and use it to help others faced with problems similar to those that I had to confront, accept, and overcome. As a survivor today, I have no hesitation in using God's divine positioning, including being Michael Jordan's sister, to inspire, encourage and educate those who feel as if they can't make it. I used to be one of them!

And, for the record, those who meet me are often left impressed by the fact that despite what my issues are and what my life plights have been, I still see the good in mankind. So though you probably did not mean it as a compliment, I gratefully embrace your labeling of me as such. Yes, TODAY, I am a happy-go-lucky woman who people love to spend time with, and I just thought you might care to know that."

As noted in Ms. Winter's catty remarks, money was often thought to be my purpose for writing about my life. Just wanting to be free of the baggage that was holding me hostage, or becoming mentally healthy, or learning to be whoever God created me to be were not deemed worthy enough causes. And then there were those who, after I had done the difficult task of writing and maneuvering the maze of publishing the book, tried cleverly to capitalize off my pain.

From using me for May's television sweeps week promotions, to shrewd businessmen seeing me as the means of making millions, many saw my pursuit for mental wellness as a means to their financial gain. Shockingly, one Pastor declared that he could see God's hands on my life and offered a million dollars to be a "lifetime" partner with me on my book, and all other business interests I would ever aspire to do. Declining his offer, I never heard from him again. Ms. Winters, however, immediately recognized her insensitivity and promptly took the time to apologize;

"Ms. Jordan, I owe you several apologies and one big 'thank you' for what occurred yesterday. My first apology comes because this note should have been written yesterday about two seconds after I received yours. I am afraid work took me away from what was the correct thing to do.

My second apology is obviously regarding the sardonic and totally inexcusable email that you received. It was, of course, never meant for you. It was a habit of ill manners from working in a newsroom where people see and hear so many bad things that smart aleck humor and bad manners becomes a way of life and a way of coping. That also is no excuse. I actually meant to forward your book e-mail to the news director because I thought it might be something he might find worthwhile. Still, there is no way I can adequately apologize, and I certainly cannot take back my bad manners and poor taste.

My last deed is to thank you or thank the 'powers that be' for letting this incident occur. It woke me up and made me realize that the smart remark made in jest can be very hurtful to someone. I certainly never meant to hurt you."

The above mocking was just one of a few incidences I confronted when I first embarked on the journey of taking ownership of my life by publicly dismantling assumptions, social ideologies, and falsehoods that were anchored in place long before I found my voice. Stumbling into the literary world through no desire of my own, I was totally convinced that God was crazy to want me to let my secrets and insecurities surface so openly.

Who in their right mind would ever do such a thing?

Having long kept a journal as my method for coping with a roller coaster of twists and turns that overwhelmed my life, I often scribbled my thoughts with all assumptions that they were for my eyes only. In that many of my personal hardships had been multiplied by my parents' and brother's popularity, I had found it difficult to enjoy all the ways their success was impacting my life. Yet, I could do nothing more than write out my feelings.

Trapped like a mouse in a maze, I had hoped that writing down my thoughts would somehow provide me greater clarity in working through my issues. How clever of God to allow my challenges to become overwhelming to the point of writing them down. He knew that He had a purpose for my efforts that reached far beyond any that I had for myself.

Still, when confronted with His steering of writing a book, I first recoiled with a mindset similar to the Biblical giant, Moses, as I proceeded to tell God all the reasons why I was not the right person for the task. Broken, beat down, and practically annihilated by a life of dysfunctions, what could I possibly say that was worth anyone hearing?

Me, who was the least of my siblings, had a life story unlike all the rest. A story that in no way would bring any positive attention to me nor my family, and would in no way support the many accounts already in circulation as to who we were as a family. But it was as if God heard all of my excuses and still refused to allow me to ignore the task. So with a mindset much like that of a rebellious child who is made to stand before their parent, but refuses to speak, I surrendered to the task of sharing my story but was more than happy to let an experienced writer ghostwrite it for me.

God, however, would not allow me to do that either!

So obvious to me now, now that I survived the task and can speak with survivor wisdom, God knew that writing my story was less about the book itself and more about the healing that would come from the journey. Degrees of healing that I could have never gained had I not walked out the process myself.

The task of just trying to put my despair in words required me to dig around in all of the messy and unpleasant places in my life to find the words that best described my heartache. And once face to face with the truth, I was forced to make peace with it.

Honestly, who else could have possibly done such a thing for me?

When hiking through a jungle, oftentimes we are drawn deeper into the wilderness of uncertainties with each step that we take. Entangled in the forest of unfamiliarities, without a clear understanding of where the pathway will take us, or what awaits us on the other side of the journey, we intuitively know that remaining lost in the jungle is not a viable option. Having started the journey and now too far in to turn around, we come to realize that it is imperative that we keep moving to avoid being swallowed up by the ferociousness of our surroundings.

What lost and frightened person takes time to appreciate the birds chirping, or the bunny rabbits hopping along the trail, when they are running for their life?

It is only after we arrive at a place of safety that we have the greatest admiration for how far we have traveled, the various sceneries we saw along the way, and the wisdom acquired from the journey. Such is the footnotes of my life with God and my literary experience.

Liberated from my life of turmoil and fears by the writing of them, I had no idea how my life would be impacted by the experience. I just knew that wherever the journey took me, it could not be any worse than where it first began. Now, many years later, I can say without shame or regret that I am so glad that I took *that* journey, and so many others, with God. As you see from the writing of this book, I am still journeying with Him and sincerely encourage you to take one with Him as well. While He may not guide you to write a book, He is sure to guide you through your dark moments while teaching you that you too are indeed stronger than your situations.

LIFE'S LESSON

The LORD is a shelter for the oppressed, a refuge in times of trouble
—Psalm 9:9 (NLT)

WHERE DO WE LEARN LIFE'S REAL LESSONS? Usually it is not when the crowds are cheering, money is in the bank, and we feel great. Rather, we learn lessons when a friend disappoints us, the job ends, the report from the doctor isn't good. It's in these difficult times that we find that we need to turn to Someone greater than ourselves.

Are you in the middle of one of those challenging times right now? First of all, know this: even when others don't understand, God does. He is here, ready right now to listen to everything that is in your heart. God is the best listener in the universe. But He is more than that. He will share life-changing truth with us if we are willing to listen. That truth can come in many forms: a phone call from a friend, a new discovery from the Bible, a circumstance with God's unmistakable fingerprints on it, a quiet internal conviction that He is speaking.

None of us enjoy going through hard times, but most of us can point back to these trials as the time when we grew the most as people. Take the journey with God and know that you will emerge triumphant.[18]

—The Authors

CHAPTER SIX

Created on Purpose For a Purpose

One evening, after a long day of busyness, I yearned to be still and enjoy the rare summer breeze. As I raised my bedroom window to let the breeze in, I soon learned that the latching mechanism that was designed to keep the window hoisted up was not working properly. Scanning around the room for a fast and immediate remedy, my eyes landed on the hammer that I had used earlier to hang a picture. Grabbing the hammer with one hand while I held the window up with the other, I quickly positioned the tool in the opening, hoping that it could support the window.

Guess what?

It worked! — It worked so well, in fact, that after double-checking it several times later to survey how it was holding up, I turned my attention to other things and left the hammer in place.

Having grabbed it initially in haste, my continual use of the tool was very much intentional. What had begun as a quick fix for my broken window grew to become my permanent solution. So much so that even when it rained, I would routinely remove the hammer to close my window so intrusive raindrops would not soak my carpet. When that threat had passed, however, I would once again raise my window and remount the tool. And when summer days turned to winter chills, I would promptly remove the hammer and store it close to its place of employment. Mindful that as sure as the cold days came, hot ones would roll around again, and so would my need to open my window again.

One day, a year or so later, as I laid stretched across my bed, my eyes wandered around the room and ultimately landed on the hammer. Lazily relaxing, with nothing pressing demanding my attention, I became fixated on the tool and began to mull over what its creator would say if he saw how I was using his creation.

Letting my thoughts roam free without any attempts to contain them, I thought about how I would feel if I were its creator; observing an instrument that I had created to be strikingly powerful in the hands of those who appreciated its strength, reduced to leaning monotonously under the weight of a broken window.

In its present role, there was nothing particularly striking or mighty about it. Although it had proven that it was indeed robust enough to handle the trivial task that it had been assigned, it was not at all functioning at its optimum capability. But without its creator around to speak specifically to his purpose for creating it, and unable to speak itself of the creator's intention, the tool was left to the task of my choosing, with its value reduced to the value that I assessed it.

Yes! Clearly I had far too much time on my hands that particular afternoon. But my time of reflection struck a nerve and I soon found myself consumed with thoughts of purpose. Especially when my thoughts turned to the window and flooded me with a whole new set of questions as I pondered how its maker might feel about the fact that although I knew it was broken, I had not even bothered to try to get it repaired.

If I was put in a position to have to explain those actions, or lack thereof, what could I say beyond admitting that I was just being lazy?

Well, maybe that's not the right word!

Truth be told, I had become preoccupied with too many other things to stop and give the damaged window my full attention. I knew when I grabbed the hammer that it was not created to prop open windows. Yet, I assigned it the task anyway and found contentment in the fact that it worked.

So what's the big deal? It wasn't like either of the creators were around to see how I was disrespecting their creations.

Then it dawned on me. If I did not think those creators would be happy with how I had dismissed and devalued their creations, what must God feel when He looks us—all of us—who He created on purpose, for a purpose?

For many of us, we have been blessed with the freedom to choose many things about our life: what we eat, what we wear, where we live, who we marry, where we go to college, where we work, and a surplus of other similar decisions. As members of the free world, these freedoms are considered the norm to us and declared to be our fundamental rights. With such being the case, many of us have come to believe that the paths that we travel in life, and the decisions we make about it, are ours alone to make. And for the most part, they are!

Woven into the infrastructure of each of our lives long before we are mindful of any personal rights, however, are intricate designs and chiseling moments that will help shape the ultimate purpose God gave us life. Until we turn to Him to learn our true value and purpose, however, many of us will continue to stumble through our existence, propping up windows when we were created to be wonderful towers of strength, fulfilling a specific and unique purpose.

Don't we owe it to our Creator to learn what that purpose is?

What might He say about what we have done with His creations—our lives?

What might He say about how we have cared for the world that He gave us?

Look around us, there are tremendous cracks in humanity and there is no way you can live in this world and not notice that.

What steps are you taking to help repair the things that are broken?

God created all of us to be vital components in this broken world. I don't think He wants any of us to just settle for being broken. Likewise, I don't think He created us to just prop up broken windows either.

Mindful of how much I had become complacent with my lounging hammer and malfunctioning window, I made the conscious decision to return them both to the tasks that best represented their creators' intentions. Then, I turned my attention to continuing to do nothing less with my life.

OVERCOME OR OVERCOMING?

I have said these things to you, that in me you may have peace. In the world you will have tribulations. But take heart; I have overcome the world.
—John 16:33 (ESV)

IT'S A FACT OF LIFE: as long as we live in this fallen world, trials, pains, and wounds are unavoidable. Our experiences will differ from others' in detail and degree. But all of us will suffer harm of some kind, likely many times along the way. We will all encounter situations that provide fertile ground for resentment and unforgiveness to take root and bloom in our hearts.

But here's another fact of life that may not be so obvious; the outcome of our lives is not determined by what happens to us or how others treat us but how we *respond* to those "hard things."

We will be affected, of course, by these painful circumstances that are a part of the fabric of our lives. But horrendous as they may be, those things do not have the power to control the outcome of who we are. They do not possess the authority to declare us *victims*.

Now this may not sound like good news, because it seems to place the burden of responsibility back on us, leaving us no one to blame for our issues. But I assure you that embracing this truth is vital in our spiritual journey.

When we as God's children realize that His grace is sufficient for every situation, at that point we are no longer victims. We are free to rise above and move on beyond whatever may have been done to us, to release those who have wronged us, and to become instruments of grace, reconciliation, and redemption in the lives of other hurting people—even in the lives of our offenders.

Yes, we can be free if we choose to be!

Counsel your heart with this truth; I do not have to be a victim or a prisoner to circumstances or people that have hurt me. By God's grace, I can walk in peace, wholeness, and joy, even in the midst of the tribulations of this world.[19]

—Nancy Leigh DeMoss

As I bring our time together to a close, I cannot end without reminding you that Jesus paid a huge price for our lives. Not because He owed us anything. Merely because He thought us to be worth the pain of the cross. So before you denounce your life, or take another step towards suicide, please spend some time with Him to learn your true value and purpose. You owe yourself that gift!

THE END OF THE STORY

THERE ARE DARK MOMENTS IN EVERY ADVENTURE. The best novels contain chapters where it looks like all hope is lost, the main character doesn't stand a chance, doom is certain. But we keep reading, don't we? We know, deep inside, that something isn't right. The picture isn't complete. Resolution will come. The hero will be okay in the end.

Reading these stories teaches us something. We can't judge the author by a single chapter. We cannot believe that the writer is a terrible person simply because the hero goes through terrible times. On the contrary, we believe that a good author won't leave the hero in despair. A good author will provide a way out.

In the same way, when we come to God, heavy with our own problems and burdened with the woes of others, we must understand that the story isn't over. We cannot take too thin a slice of life or history and try to judge God's character by it. God is ready to write the best possible ending to each person's life. If you are willing to make Him the Author of your life, He will bring you there no matter how dark your path may be in the process.[20]

—The Authors

ENDNOTES

1 Sarah Young, *Jesus Always: Embracing Joy in His Presence* (Nashville: Thomas Nelson, 2016), pg 120

2 The Authors, *Alone In God's Presence: A 365 Daily Devotional Journal* (Minneapolis: Summerside Press, 2011), Oct. 23

3 Ibid, Jan. 2

4 Sarah Young, *Jesus Always: Embracing Joy in His Presence* (Nashville: Thomas Nelson, 2016), pg 27

5 The Authors, *Alone In God's Presence: A 365 Daily Devotional Journal* (Minneapolis: Summerside Press, 2011), Jan. 24

6 Nancy Leigh DeMoss, *The Quiet Place: Daily Devotional Readings* (Chicago, Moody Publishers, 2012), Feb. 10

7   The Authors, *Alone In God's Presence: A 365 Daily Devotional Journal* (Minneapolis: Summerside Press, 2011), May 18

8   Ibid, Aug. 29

9   Nancy Leigh DeMoss, *The Quiet Place: Daily Devotional Readings* (Chicago, Moody Publishers, 2012), Jan. 22

10 The Authors, *Alone In God's Presence: A 365 Daily Devotional Journal* (Minneapolis: Summerside Press, 2011), Mar. 6

11 Sarah Young, *Jesus Always: Embracing Joy in His Presence* (Nashville: Thomas Nelson, 2016), pg 193

12 The Authors, *Alone In God's Presence: A 365 Daily Devotional Journal* (Minneapolis: Summerside Press, 2011), Jan. 18

13 Ibid, Jan. 19

14 Ibid, Jan. 14

15 Ibid, Jan. 30

16 Ibid, Nov. 27

17 Ibid, May 4

18 Ibid, Sept. 25

19 Nancy Leigh DeMoss, *The Quiet Place: Daily Devotional Readings* (Chicago, Moody Publishers, 2012), Jan. 20

20 The Authors, *Alone In God's Presence: A 365 Daily Devotional Journal* (Minneapolis: Summerside Press, 2011), Apr. 8

If you are thinking about suicide, or worried about a friend or loved one, or just would like some emotional support, the Lifeline network is available 24/7 across the United States. **Call now.**

NATIONAL

SUICIDE

PREVENTION

LIFELINE™

1-800-273-TALK (8255)

suicidepreventionlifeline.org

ABOUT THE AUTHOR

Deloris E. Jordan wears many hats, and is elated today that she has the opportunity, freedom, and mindset to choose the things that brings her joy. In addition to authoring books and being an encouragement-product line CEO, the mother of three and grandmother to five is also an inspirational speaker, minister, and licensed real estate agent. A North Carolinian native, she resides in Pennsylvania.